ENGLAND
of One Hundred Years Ago
PHOTOGRAPH COLLECTION

WEST SUSSEX

SELECTED BY AYLWIN GUILMANT

ALAN SUTTON

First published in the United Kingdom in 1992
by Alan Sutton Publishing Limited
Phoenix Mill, Stroud, Gloucestershire

First published in the United States of America
by Alan Sutton Publishing Incorporated
83 Washington Avenue, Dover, New Hampshire

British Library and Library of Congress
Cataloguing in Publication Data applied for

ISBN 0-7509-03074

Typesetting and origination by
Alan Sutton Publishing Limited
Graphics and Design Department.
Printed in Great Britain by
Bath Colour Books.

Some blemishes have been removed by extreme enlargement of the image to individual pixel
level, with careful computer graphics surgery to mend scratches, foxing, or other damage to the
photographic image.

ENGLAND
of One Hundred Years Ago
VOLUME TEN

West Sussex

The photograph collection of England of One Hundred Years Ago is an attempt to find and produce some of the best images in existence from late Victorian times up to the onset of the First World War. The country has been split into the traditional counties and this volume, numbered 10, represents West Sussex.

The criteria for selection are quality and clarity in the image together with subject interest. An attempt has been made to ensure a reasonable geographical balance within the area covered, but it has to be admitted that some areas were much more photographed than others.

The printed images are intended to be used for framing, although some people may wish to buy additional separate prints for framing by using the order form at the back of the book, and to keep this book intact. If the order form becomes separated from the book please write to the Phoenix Mill address advising the volume number and plate number you require.

The reproductions in this book are obtained by digital scanning and computer enhancement. Some blemishes have been removed by extreme enlargement of the image to individual pixel level, with careful computer graphics surgery to mend scratches,

foxing, or other damage to the photographic image. The pictures on the facing page show a scratch, enlarged and repaired. Some damage, or blemishes in an otherwise interesting photograph are beyond reasonable repair, and have been left.

The monochrome image is then further enhanced by being artificially separated and printed in a four colour process with a sepia bias. The result is a high quality image with visual depth. The finished printed image is then protected by a careful application of matt varnish to reduce fading and to add protection. The paper is a super-calendared, acid free, matt art of 170 grammes weight per square metre.

The contents of the photographs remain totally genuine and the enhancement and surgery are used only to mend damage and not to create artificial images!

West Sussex around the turn of the century was very much a rural area with many of the population working on farms or employed in coastal pursuits to do with the resorts such as Worthing and Littlehampton. The scenes portrayed here show an apparently peaceful and unhurried lifestyle, followed in small villages and towns that had yet to experience the motor car, industrialization and the social upheaval of the First World War.

Contents

Acknowledgements
Most of the photographs used in this book are reproduced
courtesy of Worthing Reference Library; the remainder are
from the compiler's own collection.

Plate 1. BOSHAM CHURCH
Bosham Church and Green, *c.* 1900

Plate 2. THE OLD MILL
North Mill at Midhurst, *c.* 1905

Plate 3. ROMANTIC RUINS
Cowdray House, Midhurst, 1905

Plate 4. A DAY IN THE SUN
Littlehampton pier and harbour, 1898

Plate 5. SPLENDOUR IN STONE
The Market Cross, Chichester, 1903

Plate 6. MIDHURST
North Street, Midhurst, 1907

Plate 7. MILL RACE
The mill at Fittleworth, 1899

Plate 8. CHICHESTER

East Street, Chichester, 1892

Plate 9. REFLECTIONS
St Mary's Church, Horsham, 1923

Plate 10. ARUNDEL CASTLE
1906

Plate 11. DELIVERED TO YOUR DOOR
Hurstpierpoint Stores and van (place unknown), *c.* 1900

Plate 12. VILLAGE GREEN
Wisborough Green, 1896

Plate 13. PLAYING IN THE LANE
Billingshurst, 1907

Plate 14. CASTLE GROUNDSMAN
Arundel Castle, 1906

Plate 15. THE VANDERBILT COACH
A wedding party outside the Plough Inn, Pycombe, *c.* 1914

Plate 16. THE GOAT CART
Beach scene at Worthing, 1903

Plate 17. MILLSTREAM
Town Mill at Horsham, 1891

Plate 18. THREE BRIDGES
Hazelwick Mill, 1906

Plate 19. LIFEBOAT PARADE
Worthing lifeboat and men in Marine Parade (date unknown)

Plate 20. WATERING THE HORSES
The church and castle at Amberley, 1906

Plate 21. THE SHEARING TEAM
Sheepshearers at work (place unknown), *c.* 1910

Plate 22. VILLAGE STORES
Handcross, c. 1905

Plate 23. VIEW FROM THE SHEEP DOWNS
Petworth, 1908

Plate 24. VILLAGE CHILDREN
Angel Street, Petworth, 1908

Plate 25. SANATORIUM GARDEN
Patients in the garden at King Edward VII Hospital, Midhurst, 1907

Plate 26. THE VICAR'S VISIT
The vicar of Keymer visiting parishioners in Lodge Lane, *c.* 1910

Plate 27. THE CARRIER'S WAGON
Outside The Anchor at Bosham, *c.* 1910

Plate 28. THE LIFEBOATMEN
Lifeboatmen at Worthing (date unknown)